Emotional intelligence is not a buzzword - it's a real game changer. And yet we learn all sorts of things at school, but not how to deal with our feelings or those of others. We practice the basics, but not how to stay calm in an argument or react empathetically in difficult conversations. Yet it is precisely these skills that are crucial for a good life.

This book was born out of a simple desire: To help people understand themselves and others better - without technical jargon, without pointing fingers, but with a lot of heart and suitability for everyday use.

Daniel Franz Albin Mittelbach has a master's degree in applied psychology, a bachelor's degree in business administration and is a qualified Quality Manager NDS HF. After more than 15 years in management positions in international companies, he now supports people and teams in their personal and professional development as a coach, trainer and consultant.

Daniel Franz Albin Mittelbach

Emotional Intelligence Made Easy

A practical book for everyday life

tredition

© 2025 Daniel Franz Albin Mittelbach
Website: https://pbc-mittelbach.com

Publishing label: Private & Business Coaching Mittelbach

Printing and distribution on behalf of the author:
tredition GmbH, Heinz-Beusen-Stieg 5, 22926 Ahrensburg, Germany

ISBN
Paperback   ISBN 978-3-384-57331-5
Hardcover   ISBN 978-3-384-57332-2
e-Book   ISBN 978-3-384-57333-9

Contact address according to EU product safety regulation:

impressumservice@tredition.com

Table of contents

Emotional intelligence - the key to a more fulfilling everyday life

E motions accompany us every day and influence our decisions, relationships and well-being. However, they often catch us at the very moments when we least expect them: when anger boils up because a colleague interrupts us in a meeting; when we feel helpless because our child is throwing a tantrum; or when we are disappointed because a good friend doesn't reply to our messages. Sometimes even completely irrelevant things make us boil.

But how often do we really consciously recognize our feelings and channel them into constructive channels? This is where emotional intelligence (EI) comes into play: it helps us to recognize and regulate our own emotions, while at the same time learning to better understand the feelings of others. The good thing is that emotional intelligence is not an innate ability, but a skill that we can practice and continuously develop. That is precisely the aim of this book.

Three typical everyday situations - How EI makes the difference

Profession: The unpleasant feedback meeting

Sophie works in a large company and has just completed an important project. During the feedback meeting with her line manager, she receives not only praise but also clear criticism. Her first impulse is to defend herself - she feels her pulse quicken and she wants to disagree. But then she thinks of an EI strategy: take a deep breath, pause for a moment and ask questions of understanding before responding. When she questions the criticism more closely, she realizes that it can actually help her to become even better at the next project.

Family: The child's tantrum

Markus comes home after a hard day at work. His four-year-old daughter screams and throws herself on the floor because she can't have ice cream for dinner. Markus feels his stress levels rising and wants to speak up. But then he remembers that a child cannot yet control their emotions as well as an adult. Instead of scolding his daughter, he kneels down, speaks to her calmly and helps her to calm down. The situation doesn't resolve immediately, but it doesn't escalate any further - because Markus has his own reaction under control.

Friendship: The misunderstanding in the WhatsApp group

Lisa is writing in a WhatsApp group with her best friend Julia and a few other friends. Suddenly Julia seems short-tempered and irritable. Lisa asks herself anxiously: "Did I say something wrong?" She feels insecurity rising inside her. But instead of being offended or withdrawing, she asks Julia calmly and without reproach whether everything is okay. Julia explains that she has had a stressful day and that her mood has nothing to do with Lisa. Problem solved before it could even become a major conflict.

Why this book?

Emotional intelligence can help us in so many areas of life - at work, in the family and among friends. It strengthens our relationships, reduces stress and leads to more informed decisions. The best thing about it is that it can be trained like a muscle. In this book you can expect, among other things:

Everyday exercises: Easy and quick to implement, so you can incorporate them into your daily routines.

Practical tips: Concrete instructions for action so that you feel an immediate change.

Reflection questions: To help you understand your own thoughts, feelings and actions more precisely and shape them accordingly.

Not only will you learn to be more aware of your own emotions, but you will also develop a deeper empathy for the feelings of those around you. This can prevent misunderstandings, defuse conflicts and help you to have authentic and fulfilling relationships.

Emotions as a source of strength

Emotional intelligence does not mean suppressing feelings or distancing ourselves from them. On the contrary, it invites us to recognize our emotions as valuable signposts. They tell us what we need right now, where our limits lie and how we can better support ourselves and others.

EI is more than just a tool for mastering difficult situations in everyday life - it is also the key to more self-care, empathy and authentic interaction.

Are you ready to become more aware of your feelings and use them constructively instead of letting them overwhelm you? Then let's embark on this journey together and strengthen your emotional intelligence step by step.

Have fun discovering and applying the upcoming tips and exercises!

What is emotional intelligence? Why emotional intelligence is more important than you think

"People are hired for their professional competence - and fired for their behavior."

It's an often quoted saying that aptly describes how important it is to deal with our own and other people's feelings in everyday life.

E motion intelligence is one of the most valuable skills we can develop in life. It not only affects our private lives but also shapes our professional success and the way we work together. The way we deal with stress, conflict and change. Those who know and can control their emotions stay calmer, make clearer decisions and build more sustainable relationships.

Just think of a situation in which you felt unfairly treated - perhaps at work or in an argument with a friend. Reacting in an emotionally intelligent way doesn't mean suppressing your feelings but being aware of them and dealing with them constructively. Instead of becoming impulsive, you can seek a conversation, show understanding for the other person's perspective and look for a solution together.

The five pillars of emotional intelligence

The psychologist Daniel Goleman has made the concept of emotional intelligence tangible through five central competencies.

The five core competencies initially include **self-awareness,** i.e. the ability to clearly recognize and understand your own emotions. If you know what you are feeling and why, you can influence your feelings in a meaningful way in the next step - and this is exactly where **self-regulation** comes in. It describes the conscious handling of emotions, which involves avoiding impulsive behavior. Instead of letting yourself be overwhelmed by anger or frustration, for example, you can learn to take a step back internally and look for constructive solutions.

Building on this, **motivation** plays a central role. It describes the ability to inspire oneself and continue to pursue goals even when obstacles arise. People with a high level of emotional intelligence often manage to overcome setbacks and reorient themselves from crises.

An equally important factor is **empathy,** i.e. understanding the feelings and needs of others. Those who can empathize with their counterparts enable harmonious cooperation, recognize potential conflicts early on and treat others with respect and appreciation.

The whole thing is rounded off by **social skills,** which are demonstrated when we actively shape relationships, communicate clearly and empathetically and successfully resolve conflicts. This includes aspects such as assertiveness, team spirit and a polite tone - even (and especially) when situations become difficult. These five aspects form the basis for a high level of emotional intelligence, which benefits us in all areas of life.

Emotional quotient (EQ) vs. intelligence quotient (IQ)

Many people assume that a high IQ is the key to success. Of course, cognitive skills such as analysis and problem solving are important. But how we work in teams, react under pressure or anticipate customer requirements depends largely on our "EQ". Studies show that emotional intelligence often makes the decisive difference as to whether we can hold our own in complex social situations or not.

A high level of emotional intelligence enables us to manage stress more effectively, defuse conflicts and maintain authentic relationships. Those who master these skills not only work more productively but also develop a stronger sense of self-efficacy and satisfaction - both at work and in their private lives.

Why emotional intelligence can be learned

The good news is that emotional intelligence is not innate and fixed, but a skill that we can develop - much like a muscle that we train. This means that each of us can increase our EQ, regardless of age, level of education or life situation. The decisive factors are practice and a willingness to deal with your own feelings.

In the following chapters, you will learn practical strategies and exercises to deal with your emotions more consciously, reduce stress and strengthen your relationships. The aim is not to become 'perfect' or to avoid every negative emotion. Rather, the aim is to find a healthy and mature way of dealing with all emotions - your own and those of others.

Concrete everyday examples

At work: Imagine your boss criticizes your work. Instead of reacting angrily or withdrawing, you could question your initial reaction ("Why do I feel attacked?") and seek a conversation to get constructive feedback.

In the family: When siblings argue, empathy helps to understand the emotions of both parties. This allows you to mediate instead of getting angry yourself.

Between friends: If a friend is often late, open but understanding communication is more likely to lead to a solution than if you are just annoyed or reproach her.

Reflection questions for you

- **When was the last time you experienced a situation in which you reacted emotionally?**
  How would you have acted with more emotional intelligence?
- **Are there certain emotions that you particularly struggle with?**

What could be the first steps to better understand these emotions?

- **How do you normally deal with stress and conflict?**
  Can you imagine using strategies to help you stay calmer?

Take a moment to think about these questions. They will help you to better assess your starting position and recognize which areas of your emotional intelligence you would particularly like to develop further.

What next?

Now that you know the basics of emotional intelligence, let's dive deeper into each area together. In the next chapter, you will get to know the first skill - **self-awareness** - in more detail and learn how to develop a finer sense of your own feelings.

Let's start with a look inside yourself - because before we can understand others, we first have to understand ourselves.

To the point

- **Definition**: EI involves recognizing, understanding and directing one's own feelings and those of others.
- **5 core competencies according to Goleman:**
    - Self-awareness
    - Self-regulation
    - Motivation
    - Empathy
    - Social skills
- **IQ vs. EQ**: Professional competence is important, but dealing with emotions and relationships is often more decisive for long-term success.
- **Learnable**: EI is not a talent, but a skill that anyone can train.
- **Reflection questions**: Be aware of situations in which you react emotionally - and consider how EI can help.

Self-awareness - Understanding yourself better

Before we can regulate our emotions or understand the emotions of others, we must learn to consciously perceive our own emotions. Self-awareness means recognizing which emotions we feel, why we feel them and how they influence our behavior. It is the starting point for creating constructive relationships in the long term - both with us and with others. Because only when we understand what moves us at our core can we react to it and steer our emotions in a beneficial direction.

Strategies for improving self-awareness

Naming emotions

Although we are often aware of our feelings, we often avoid naming them specifically - perhaps out of fear of "revealing" ourselves. However, consciously identifying and naming our own emotions is the first step towards a clearer understanding of ourselves.

Interpreting body signals

Emotions are not only expressed in our thoughts, but also physically: palpitations, tension, a lump in the throat or butterflies in the stomach are all indications of how we are feeling. If you learn to recognize these signals, you will notice more quickly when certain feelings are brewing.

Reflection through journaling

Keeping a diary (analogue or digital) helps you to recognize emotional patterns. Write down briefly and regularly what you have experienced and how it made you feel. In this way, you can better classify and understand triggers for certain emotions.

Get feedback from others

Other people sometimes perceive our feelings more clearly than we do ourselves. By talking to friends, colleagues or family members, we can gain new perspectives on our own behavior. It is important to be open to criticism and input from outside.

Conscious self-observation

Take regular moments of silence or mindfulness - for example, when you're out walking, cooking or in the shower. Ask yourself: "How am I feeling right now?" and listen to yourself. These conscious time-outs help you to distance yourself from hectic situations and sharpen your awareness of inner processes.

Anna and the underlying irritation

Recently, Anna had noticed more and more often that she reacted irritably to the smallest of things. She often came home from work in the evening and felt an inner restlessness - for no specific reason. One day, when her partner just asked her if she had collected the post yet, she literally shot off: "I can decide that for myself!"

In hindsight, she realized that her outburst actually had little to do with this simple question. She realized that she had already felt this pulling in her chest and the shallow breathing on the way home. She was simply tired and stressed without consciously realizing it. After Anna took the time to journal for ten minutes in the evening and name her feelings, she realized that her body had been sending her signals much earlier. Now that she was more aware of these warning signs, she was able to take targeted countermeasures - such as a short breathing exercise or a clarifying conversation about her working day.

Practical exercises for self-awareness

Keep an emotional diary

Write down your most intense feelings and their triggers every day. Make a note of when they occur and how your body reacts. After just a few days, you will recognize certain patterns or recurring situations that particularly affect you.

Mindfulness meditation

Mindfulness meditation focuses on the present moment. Sit comfortably, breathe calmly and notice what is going on inside you - without judging. In this way, you learn to notice feelings even when they are still quietly knocking.

Body scan

Close your eyes and direct your attention from your feet to your head through your whole body. Try to feel tension, warmth, cold or tingling sensations. These sensations will give you an indication of how you are feeling emotionally and strengthen your body awareness.

Feelings naming exercise

Make a list of emotional terms (there are numerous "emotional lists" on the internet). When you notice that you are feeling something, try to find the right term. This will expand your "emotional vocabulary" and create clarity.

Reflection questions

- **What emotions do you experience most often?**
  Do pleasant or unpleasant feelings predominate? Do you have the feeling that certain emotions come up again and again in similar situations?
- **Are there any triggers that have a particularly strong influence on you?**

Notice whether certain people, places or tasks put you in a certain mood. Perhaps a tight schedule leads to stress, while praise from your boss immediately triggers feelings of happiness.

- **How do your emotions change your behavior?**
  Do you get loud when you're angry or do you tend to withdraw? How do the people around you react? You may discover valuable clues here about how your behavior shapes your relationships.

- **What does a certain emotion tell me about my needs or values?**
  For example, anger could be based on an unfulfilled need for recognition, sadness on a feeling of loss. If you recognize this, you can react to it in a targeted way.

Self-acceptance as a basis

Self-awareness means not only recognizing what feelings we have but also accepting them. It is normal to feel angry, sad or frustrated sometimes. Feelings are important signposts and tell us what is going well or not so well in our lives. When we accept ourselves, we create a secure basis for dealing with our emotions - and thus the foundation for healthy emotional growth.

To the point

- **Why self-awareness**? Without clarity about your own feelings, targeted control is not possible.
- **Central strategies**:
    - Naming emotions
    - Interpreting body signals
    - Journaling (keeping a diary)
    - Accepting feedback from others
    - Conscious self-observation
- **Practical exercises**: Emotion diary, mindfulness meditation, body scan.
- **Reflection questions**: Which emotions arise frequently? What are typical triggers? What are the underlying needs?

Self-regulation - consciously controlling emotions

E Having emotions is deeply human. However, what makes the big difference is the way we deal with our emotions. Self-regulation does not mean suppressing or ignoring emotions but consciously directing them. This helps us to avoid impulsive reactions, remain confident in stressful situations and maintain our inner balance. We develop the ability to influence our reactions in a targeted manner - and can thus shape relationships, everyday working life and personal goals in a more positive way.

Leon's erratic car journey

Leon had just had an argument with a colleague. Angry, he got into his car and wanted to drive home quickly. Before he had even left the parking lot, he realized that his heart was pounding and his hands on the steering wheel were getting clammy. He almost rear-ended a van because his thoughts were constantly revolving around the argument.

Then he remembered what he had recently read about self-regulation. He stopped for a moment, took three deep breaths and asked himself: "What do I actually need now?" He realized that he didn't want to stay angry, he wanted to get home safely. So he decided to switch on a quieter radio station and put the argument aside for the moment. The rest of the journey was much more relaxed and when he arrived home, he was able to clarify his concerns more objectively.

Strategies for self-regulation

Various approaches can help you to consciously control your emotions and avoid impulsive reactions. One particularly effective method is working with **breathing techniques**. Deep, conscious breaths calm the body and provide a moment of clarity. The 4-4-4 method, for example, has proven effective here: This involves breathing in for four seconds, pausing briefly and then breathing out for four seconds. Regularly practicing these breathing pauses makes it easier to stay calm even in moments of acute stress.

Another important component of self-regulation **is reframing**. Our personal assessment of a situation has a significant influence on how we feel about it. It can therefore help to specifically ask yourself: "What else could be positive or helpful about this situation?" This conscious change of perspective makes it possible to transform anger or fear into curiosity or a focus on solutions.

It is also helpful to recognize typical emotional triggers. If you are aware of which topics or situations upset you particularly quickly, you can take countermeasures earlier. A "**trigger diary**" is suitable for this, in which you note down exactly when strong feelings occur and why. Those who know their personal triggers generally react more confidently and can cope better with stressful moments.

Finally, it is advisable to develop your own **self-calming strategies**. Whether it's music, yoga, a walk, mindfulness exercises or even just short breaks in everyday life - everyone has their own individual ways of restoring inner calm. Small rituals such as a cup of tea, a few pages in a book or a brief moment of silence can go a long way. The key is to have a suitable "emergency strategy" to hand as soon as you feel strong feelings coming up. This way, you can remain capable of acting even in emotionally challenging situations and maintain your inner balance.

Practical exercises

The 10-second rule

Before you react in an emotionally charged situation, pause for ten seconds. Focus your attention on your breathing, feel your body and then make a conscious decision about how you want to respond.

Emotion control diary

Make a daily note of situations in which you consciously controlled your emotions. What helped you to do this? How did you feel afterwards? A diary makes progress visible and motivates you to keep at it.

Mini meditation or mindfulness moment

Take a minute or two in between to close your eyes for a moment and just observe your breathing. This helps to stop the carousel of thoughts and recharge your batteries.

Reflection questions

- **When was the last time you reacted impulsively?**
  What were your feelings and thoughts? How could you have reacted instead at that moment to protect yourself and others?
- **Which self-regulation techniques work best for you?**
  What has already proved successful and where do you still have potential to try out new things?
- **How do you feel when you control your emotions more consciously?**
  Pay attention to whether you feel calmer and clearer overall when you use self-regulation practices.

Self-regulation is a process that requires patience and regular practice. Every small change - be it a deep breath or consciously refraining from a rash reaction - contributes to greater serenity and contentment in everyday life. By lovingly accepting your emotions and learning to manage them, you not only gain inner stability, but also more clarity in your decisions and actions.

To the point

- **Definition**: Not suppression, but targeted control of emotions.
- **Benefits**: Reduce impulsive behavior, remain more confident in stressful situations.
- **Strategies**:
    - Breathing techniques (e.g. 4-4-4 method)
    - Reframing (reinterpreting thoughts)
    - Recognizing and preventing triggers
    - Self-soothing (music, walks, short breaks)
- **Practical exercises**: 10-second rule, diary for emotion control, mini-meditation.
- **Reflection questions**: When was the last time I reacted impulsively? Which self-regulation techniques help me best?

Motivation - Driving yourself forward

Motivation is the inner motor that helps us to pursue our goals and overcome challenges. It makes us stay on the ball despite setbacks. A distinction is made between **extrinsic motivation**, which arises from external incentives such as rewards or pressure, and **intrinsic motivation**, which comes from within, for example from personal interest or enjoyment of a task.

Emotional intelligence helps us to recognize and harness the power of intrinsic motivation. By becoming aware of our feelings and learning to deal with them positively, we can remain motivated in the long term.

The link between emotions and motivation

Our emotions influence how strongly we are attracted to or repelled by something. Positive emotions such as joy, enthusiasm or curiosity give us energy and make us more open to new challenges. Negative emotions such as fear, frustration or insecurity, on the other hand, can slow us down or even paralyze us.

An important step towards more self-motivation is to recognize these feelings and manage them constructively. For example, if you feel anxious, you can try to redirect your fear into curiosity or anticipation by focusing on opportunities and learning possibilities. This often turns a blockage into a drive.

Paula's marathon project

Paula had resolved to run a half marathon in five months. At first, she was full of enthusiasm, but after a few weeks' doubts began to set in. She thought: "What's the point? It's cold outside and I could just stay at home." One evening, she realized that she felt bad because she had skipped a training session.

Then she remembered the reasons for her goal: she didn't just want to get fitter, she also wanted to show that she could focus on a goal. She recalled the feeling of how proud she would be if she really persevered and stood at the starting line. "You can do it," she told herself, and you've already come so far." The next day, she went out despite the rain - and felt great afterwards. This deep, inner "why" kept her motivated, even when external circumstances (weather, lack of time) spoke against it.

Strategies for self-motivation

Strategies for self-motivation are a key component of emotional intelligence. The first step is to set goals that appeal emotionally to. By asking yourself why you really care about a particular project, you can find out what needs and values are behind it. This strengthens your inner drive and helps you to stay motivated even in the face of setbacks. It is just as important to **consciously experience success**. Even small steps forward, such as solving an everyday problem or having a successful conversation, deserve recognition. Celebrating and documenting them strengthens your self-confidence and creates a reliable source of energy for new challenges.

Another decisive factor is **positive self-talk**. Pay attention to your inner voice and replace sentences like "I can never do it" with "I grow with every challenge". By encouraging yourself, you will boost your stamina and appear more self-confident. Your environment also plays a major role: **surround yourself with positive people** who encourage you, give you constructive feedback and instill confidence. Such a supportive community can have a contagious effect and help you move forward.

It is also advisable to **develop routines,** as discipline and regularity are often more sustainable than sheer willpower. Fixed times for important tasks or sporting activities create structure in everyday life and make it easier to keep going. At the same time, you should learn to **consciously manage negative emotions.** If you feel anxious or frustrated, take a moment to feel inside yourself: what is really behind these feelings? An open conversation with a trusted person, a walk in the fresh air or consciously reflecting on your thoughts can help you to calm down and look ahead again. In this way, you can keep track of your emotions instead of letting them overwhelm you - and create the best conditions for sustainable self-motivation.

Everyday examples of emotional motivation

Career: A difficult project is more motivating when you realize what personal meaning it has for you. Ask yourself: "What can I learn from this and how will it help me move forward?"

Family/health: Sport is easier if you associate it with positive feelings, such as the fun of exercise or the good feeling after training.

Friendships: Shared goals with friends (e.g. planning a trip) increase commitment and the joy of preparation.

Practical exercises

Create vision board

Collect images, quotes and keywords that illustrate your long-term goals and wishes. Place your vision board in a place where you will see it every day.

Morning reflection

Write down three things every morning that you look forward to or are grateful for. This directs your focus to the positive and increases your basic motivation.

Self-motivation through music

Put together a playlist that gets you going and puts you in a good mood. Music can quickly influence emotions and get you back on track when you're feeling low.

Mini breaks to take a deep breath

Consciously take short breaks to meditate or stretch and stretch. This will give you new energy and prevent you from getting lost in negative thought spirals.

Reflection questions

- **What goals are you currently pursuing?**
  Are they more intrinsically or extrinsically motivated?
- **When was the last time you felt really motivated?**
  What was the trigger for this?
- **Which emotions support your motivation - and which ones slow you down?**
  How can you strengthen beneficial feelings and constructively transform hindering feelings?

If you regularly check what motivates you and which emotions support or slow you down, you can learn to use your inner source of energy effectively. Emotional intelligence helps you to recognize, accept and use your feelings in a positive way - and this is exactly what makes you more successful and satisfied in the long term.

To the point

- **Why motivation is part of EI**: Emotions determine whether we approach tasks with enthusiasm or feel blocked.
- **Intrinsic vs. extrinsic**: True perseverance usually comes from an inner drive (passion, sense of purpose).
- **Strategies**:
    - Set goals that are personally meaningful
    - Consciously recognizing and celebrating successes
    - Positive self-talk (redirect inner critic)
    - Exchange with supportive people
    - Establish routines to maintain momentum
- **Practical exercises**: Vision board, gratitude diary, self-rewards, music to lift your mood.
- **Reflection questions**: What goals am I currently pursuing? What keeps me motivated?

Empathy - understanding others better

E mpathy means empathizing with the emotions and thoughts of others and taking them seriously. It is essential for interpersonal relationships because it reduces misunderstandings, builds trust and can defuse conflicts. People with a high level of empathy perceive the feelings of others more accurately and react appropriately to them - be it through a sympathetic ear, supportive words or concrete assistance. At the same time, empathy helps people to better question their own behavior and consciously work towards greater understanding and consideration in everyday life.

The three levels of empathy

The three levels of empathy can be divided into cognitive, emotional and compassionate empathy. **Cognitive empathy** describes the ability to understand the thoughts and perspectives of others. An example of this is a situation in which you observe a colleague in a meeting who is visibly uncomfortable because he does not dare to express his opinion out of respect for his superior. Through cognitive empathy, you recognize his inhibitions and can understand them.

Emotional empathy goes beyond purely intellectual empathy in that it involves actually feeling with the emotions of others. Imagine your friend is very sad and you feel this sadness too. You can empathize with what she is going through and share her emotional distress on an emotional level.

Finally, there is **compassionate empathy**, where you actively act on the understanding you have gained. An example of this would be when you notice that a friend is having financial difficulties. You don't just offer them comfort or words of encouragement but also support them in a very concrete way - for example by connecting them with the right contacts or offering them a little financial bridging assistance. It is this willingness to act that makes compassionate empathy so valuable and shows how deep your understanding of the other person actually goes.

How empathy improves our everyday lives

Job: An empathetic boss not only notices when an employee is stressed but also asks specifically how they can help. This increases job satisfaction and trust in the team.

Family: Understanding children's emotions helps to resolve conflicts calmly. By taking the time to really understand the child, they can express their feelings better and feel taken seriously.

Friendships: Empathy prevents minor disputes from escalating. Instead of justifying yourself or jumping to conclusions, ask what has hurt the other person and try to find a solution together.

Society: Being open to the feelings and needs of others - such as neighbors, new colleagues or strangers - contributes to respectful and supportive coexistence.

Lara's new teammate

Lara got a new team colleague, Vincent, who always seemed quiet and never came into the break room. His colleagues were already whispering: "He's probably a loner or arrogant." Lara decided to ask him directly if everything was OK. She realized that Vincent was shy and felt uncomfortable at first because he didn't know anyone.

Instead of avoiding him, Lara deliberately "took him by the hand" at the next team meeting: she asked him to express his opinion on the topics and talked about his hobbies during the coffee break. Vincent was visibly relieved. Lara's emphatic approach helped him to thaw out - and he quickly integrated into the group. Looking back, Lara said: "I realized that it's not difficult for me to put myself in his shoes as soon as I'm really interested."

Strategies for strengthening empathy

Active listening is an important basis for more empathy. By listening attentively to the other person, asking comprehension questions and summarizing what has been said in your own words, you show that you really listen and understand. It is also a good idea to practice **changing perspectives**: Consciously ask yourself how the other person is feeling and what their worries or joys are. This will teach you to look at situations from their point of view.

Another essential factor is **interpreting non-verbal signals**. Facial expressions, gestures and tone of voice can often reveal more than words. If you pay careful attention to these signals, you can usually recognize the other person's feelings more quickly and accurately. **Self-reflection** is just as important: examine your own prejudices and beliefs, because only if you are aware of your attitudes can you really approach other people with an open mind.

Finally, you should also make sure to **maintain boundaries**. Empathy does not mean taking on the problems of others completely. Protect your own emotional health by only offering as much help as you can provide yourself without overburdening yourself.

Practical empathy exercises

Daily reflection

Take a few minutes in the evening to recall situations in which empathy was required. Think about what went well and where you could react even more empathetically.

Empathy exercises

Make a conscious effort to adopt the other person's point of view in every conversation for one day. Make a note of how this affects your interaction.

Reading or listening to other people's stories

Novels, biographies and interviews provide insights into other people's lives. The more you know about the experiences of others, the easier it is for you to understand their situation.

Seek personal discussions

Exchange ideas with people who have different backgrounds or perspectives. Common interests or goals can often be found more quickly than expected.

Practicing empathic communication

During a conflict discussion, try to use specific "I" messages ("I feel ... when you say/act ...") to signal to your counterpart that you are not attacking, but seeking understanding.

Reflection questions

- **When was the last time you experienced a situation in which you were particularly empathetic?**
  Think about what exactly made this situation so special: Was it the context, the person or your mood on that day?
- **Are there people or groups with whom you find it difficult to empathize? Why is that?**
  Question whether prejudices, lack of contact or negative experiences are inhibiting your empathy.
- **How can you improve your empathy in your everyday life?**
  Find small steps that help you to be more empathetic, e.g. consciously praising a person every day, wanting to understand instead of judging, or regularly taking time to actively listen.

Empathy is more than just compassion - it is a fundamental attitude that deepens our relationships and enriches our interactions. Through regular practice and awareness of the feelings of others, we can gradually create a more empathetic, understanding environment. In this way, empathy becomes a powerful key that not only opens doors to other people but also provides new insights into us.

To the point

- **Meaning**: Empathy builds bridges, reduces conflict and promotes genuine connection.
- **Three levels**:
    - Cognitive empathy (understanding thoughts/perspectives)
    - Emotional empathy (sympathizing with feelings)
    - Compassionate empathy (action-oriented support)
- **Benefits in everyday life**: resolving conflicts, deeper understanding of fellow human beings, improved working atmosphere, family life and friendships.
- **Strategies**: Active listening, changing perspective, interpreting non-verbal signals, reflecting on own prejudices, maintaining boundaries.
- **Reflection questions**: When was the last time I was particularly empathetic? With whom do I find empathy difficult?

Social skills - successful communication and relationships

S ocial competence is far more than just politeness or the ability to engage in conversation with others. It describes the ability to interact effectively with others, maintain healthy relationships and resolve conflicts constructively. Empathy plays a major role in this, but social competence goes one step further: those who are socially competent not only recognize emotions and moods in themselves and others but can also react appropriately and consciously adapt their own behavior.

Key factors of social competence

Social competence encompasses various skills, all of which are aimed at interacting effectively with others, building relationships and resolving conflicts constructively. One of these is **communication skills**: clear and respectful communication is at the heart of every relationship. Those who actively listen and formulate precisely avoid misunderstandings and create an atmosphere of mutual respect. **Conflict resolution** is just as important, as tensions and differences of opinion are normal when working together. However, the decisive factor is how we deal with them: Addressing conflicts constructively and looking for solutions together promotes a positive atmosphere and strengthens mutual trust.

Another key factor is **assertiveness**. Representing your own needs and interests without offending or ignoring others is a fundamental skill in both professional and private life. Equally important is the **ability to cooperate** whether in a team or in the family - common goals can only be achieved if everyone works together and supports each other. Finally, the **ability to express emotions** also plays a major role: expressing and showing feelings in an understandable way creates closeness and understanding in relationships. Communicating your emotions clearly while considering the sensitivities of others lay the foundation for respectful, harmonious relationships.

Sam's family weekend

Sam wanted to have a quiet weekend. His sister Anna, on the other hand, had planned to get all her siblings together and spend the night in their parents' apartment. When Sam found out about this, he was frustrated: "I want my peace and quiet, why do I have to go to another big family reunion?"

Instead of sulking or simply canceling, Sam called Anna and said: "I need your advice - I feel exhausted and need a rest. But at the same time, I don't want to let the family down. Do you have any idea how we can reconcile this?" Anna was surprised by the direct approach. Together they found a compromise: Sam would only join them on Saturday evenings and Anna would make sure he had a quiet guest room where he could retreat. Thanks to open communication, Sam felt respected, and the family atmosphere remained relaxed.

How social skills enrich our everyday lives

Profession: In everyday working life, social skills enable productive teamwork and a constructive working atmosphere. Misunderstandings are less frequent, and conflicts can be resolved more quickly.

Family: Open and respectful discussions contribute to a harmonious relationship and strengthen mutual trust.

Friendships: Those who are empathetic and strong communicators can maintain a friendly atmosphere and resolve conflicts at an early stage.

Strategies for improving social skills

Strategies for improving social skills start with **active listening**. This involves not only hearing what is being said but also paying attention to what the other person really means and feels. Regular questions signal genuine interest and promote deeper understanding. Another tool is the use **of "I" messages**: Instead of saying "You always do ...", for example, it is often more helpful to formulate "I feel ... when ...". This avoids blame and enables a constructive exchange.

In heated discussions, it is also advisable to **use de-escalation techniques**. Staying calm, taking a deep breath and taking care to regulate your own emotions creates the basis for objective and solution-oriented communication. A friendly look, open **body language** and inviting gestures underline your interest in the other person and promote a respectful discussion atmosphere. Finally, it is crucial to give and accept feedback. **Constructive feedback** not only contributes to your own development but also strengthens the relationship of trust and the relationship with the other person.

Practical exercises for more social skills

Mirror exercise

Stand in front of the mirror and consciously pay attention to your facial expressions and posture. How do you look to others?

Role-playing games

Practicing difficult conversational situations in a familiar group or in coaching. This makes it easier to stay calm and react confidently in real conflicts.

Self-reflection

After every important conversation or argument, pause for a moment and think: "What went well? What could I do better next time?"

Advanced exercises and tips

Change of perspective: Try to look at a situation from the other person's point of view. This promotes empathy and understanding.

Setting boundaries: Social competence also means communicating your own boundaries clearly and respecting the boundaries of others.

Small gestures in everyday life: an honest compliment, an attentive question or a friendly "thank you" can go a long way towards positive interaction.

Reflection questions

- **Which social situations are particularly easy for you? Which ones are more difficult?**
  In which specific situations do I notice that I am naturally open and self-confident, and where do I tend to feel tense or insecure? What could be the reason for this?
- **How good are you at staying calm and arguing objectively in heated discussions?**
  What are my typical physical and mental signs that I am becoming emotional, and how can I counteract this myself at the moment to remain calm and objective?
- **Think of a difficult situation from your past: would a different form of communication have helped you to solve the problem better?**
  If I were in the same situation today, what other words or approach would I choose to approach my counterpart more constructively?
- **When do you feel particularly comfortable in a conversation and why?**
  What external and internal factors (e.g. location, atmosphere, trust) contribute to me feeling completely accepted and understood in a conversation?
- **How do you deal with criticism - are you open to it, or do you tend to react defensively?**
  How do I sense whether I am having defensive thoughts at the moment, and at what moment could I consciously pause to see criticism as a learning opportunity rather than a personal attack?

Social competence means shaping relationships consciously and respectfully. Learning to communicate constructively, resolve conflicts empathetically and remain authentic creates an environment in which everyone involved feels comfortable. With the strategies and exercises presented, social skills can be developed step by step - for the benefit of all.

To the point

- **Why important**: Good communication and conflict resolution skills are essential for harmonious relationships.
- **Elements of social competence**:
    - Communication skills
    - Conflict resolution
    - Assertiveness
    - Willingness to cooperate
    - Emotional expression
- **Strategies**:
    - Active listening and I-messages
    - De-escalation techniques
    - Using body language consciously
    - Giving and accepting feedback
- **Practical exercises**: Role play, mirror exercise (body language), self-reflection after difficult conversations.
- **Reflection questions**: Which conversations work well? How do I deal with criticism?

Emotional intelligence in the digital world

I n an increasingly digitalized world, a large part of our communication takes place via emails, messenger services and social media. Face-to-face conversations are often replaced by short messages that lack facial expressions, gestures and tone of voice. This is exactly where misunderstandings lurk: Emotions are not always recognized correctly or can be misinterpreted. Emotional intelligence is therefore also indispensable in the digital space. It helps us to be more aware of our own feelings and those of others and to respond to them empathetically - even if we only have a smartphone or computer screen in front of us.

The challenges of digital communication

A lack of non-verbal signals is one of the biggest challenges in digital communication. As facial expressions, gestures and tone of voice are often not visible or audible, misunderstandings can quickly arise Irony and sarcasm are easily overlooked or misinterpreted. In addition, many people **react quickly instead of responding thoughtfully**. The low inhibition threshold to respond directly to messages results in spontaneous, often ill-considered reactions that can lead to heated discussions.

Another aspect is the **anonymity and distance** that is particularly pronounced in chats or social media. Under the cloak of anonymity, the inhibition threshold for a disrespectful tone is lowered, which one would probably avoid in a personal conversation. In addition, we are faced with the challenge of a veritable **information overload**: a constantly growing number of messages and posts can lead to us reading only superficially and overlooking important information.

Cultural differences in the global network should also not be underestimated. What is considered polite in one language may be perceived as impolite in another. Although cultural diversity offers many opportunities for exchange and networking, it also increases the risk of misunderstandings if you do not consciously pay attention to how your communication is received by the other person.

Luisa's short-circuit answer

Luisa was annoyed by her colleague, who was constantly sending her emails with seemingly nonsensical questions. One morning, before her first coffee, she received another request: "Where can I find the information from yesterday?" Luisa rolled her eyes and typed frantically: "It's all in the database, just look it up yourself."

Before she could click on "Send", she remembered the rule of thumb to read through emails again. She realized that her tone came across as dismissive and rude. So, she took a deep breath and rephrased: "Hi Nina, you can find the information in the database under 'Projects - Q4'. If it's still unclear, please let me know." This small change kept the atmosphere collegial. When Nina thanked her, Luisa found out that Nina's computer had an older version of the database, and she couldn't actually see everything.

Strategies for more emotional intelligence in the digital world

In digital communication, it is particularly important to **use conscious and empathetic language**. It helps to read every message carefully first and ask yourself whether the wording could be misleading before sending it. A second glance is often enough to prevent misunderstandings. When using **emojis**, less is more. Although they can help to express feelings and prevent misinterpretations, they should be used sparingly and carefully so that they do not lose their impact. Regular offline time is also useful. A "**digital detox**" creates distance from smartphones and computers and enables a more mindful approach to digital media and one's own emotions.

When it comes to **writing critical messages,** it is advisable to give constructive feedback rather than impulsive criticism. A polite form of address and specific examples of suggestions for improvement contribute to an appreciative relationship. It is also important to **remain empathetic** online. Consciously put yourself in the other person's shoes and show understanding, especially on social media.

Kind words, consideration and a **respectful tone go** a long way towards keeping discussions constructive. Finally, netiquette should always be observed: Using "please" and "thank you" or a friendly form of address will encourage respectful communication and avoid unnecessary tension.

Examples from everyday life

Profession: An email with critical content should be formulated in a factual and friendly manner. A short note such as "I look forward to your feedback" or "Thank you for your time" can significantly improve the atmosphere.

Family: A short, choppy text can quickly come across as rude. Sometimes a phone call or voice message is more personal and avoids misunderstandings.

Friendships: Arguments via Messenger often escalate because the tone of voice is lacking. A clarifying face-to-face conversation prevents negative emotions from escalating.

Practical exercises for more digital emotional intelligence

Reflect news

Read through your message again before you send it. How might it come across to the recipient? Would you say it the same way in a personal conversation?

Schedule digital detox days

Regularly switch off your smartphone or consciously put it to one side. Use the time you gain to question your digital habits and make them more conscious.

Promote positive communication

Consciously send encouraging messages: A word of praise or a kind word can brighten up everyone's everyday digital life.

Reflection questions

- **Have you ever received a message that you completely misunderstood? What led to this misinterpretation?**
  Can you remember a situation in which you completely misinterpreted a message? What factors - for example, the way it was worded, your own mood or a lack of contextual information - do you think contributed to this misunderstanding?

- **When was the last time you overreacted digitally? What could you have done differently?**
  What do you think you could have done better about your reaction or the way you expressed your feelings to defuse the situation?

- **How can you communicate more consciously and empathetically online? Is there a set routine that helps you to do this (e.g. always wait 30 seconds before sending)?**
  What specific steps or routines can you think of to pause for a moment and think about your words before sending a message - for example, a 30-second window or a short breathing space?

Emotional intelligence in the digital space is not a luxury, but a necessary skill to communicate respectfully and with understanding in an increasingly networked world. By taking our time, consciously reading and writing and responding empathetically to others, we also create an online environment that is characterized by respect, openness and positive interaction. Ultimately, we all benefit when digital communication is enriched by mindfulness, kindness and genuine interest in the other person.

To the point

- **Why relevant**: A large part of our communication takes place via chats, emails and social media - where tone of voice and facial expressions are missing.
- **Challenges**:
  - Missing non-verbal signals (misunderstandings)
  - Fast, impulsive reactions
  - Anonymity and distance can make respect more difficult
  - Information overload
- **Strategies**:
  - Conscious reading/writing (check message before sending)
  - Use emojis sensibly
  - Take digital breaks
  - Observe netiquette (asking, thanking, politeness)
- **Practical exercises**: Pausing before sending, mindful use of social media, encouraging positive online communication.
- **Reflection questions**: How can I avoid misunderstandings online? Which online habits are not good for me?

Practical exercises for everyday life

EMotion intelligence is not an innate, unchangeable characteristic, but an ability that can be improved through training. Similar to learning an instrument or playing sport, only repeated, conscious practice leads to noticeable progress. If you regularly make time for the following exercises, you will continuously develop and deepen your self-awareness, self-regulation, empathy and social skills.

Lena's evening routine

Lena had long working days and was often stressed when she got home. Simple little things, such as doing the dishes, drove her up the wall. When she read that just five minutes of mindfulness practice could significantly reduce her stress, she was skeptical - but gave it a try.

Every evening, she sat down briefly with a cup of tea, closed her eyes and concentrated only on her breathing. After a few days, she noticed that she became calmer and no longer reacted so impulsively in the evening. Her evening routine (tea + 5 minutes of mindfulness) became a regular habit. Now she often looks back happily and says: "These five minutes of breathing space have totally changed the way I feel after work."

Exercises for self-awareness

Solid self-awareness forms the basis for all other areas of emotional intelligence. If you are aware of your feelings and physical reactions, you can control and understand your emotions in a more targeted way.

Keep an emotional diary

Every evening, write down three emotions that you felt during the day and reflect on what triggered them. Also make a brief note of how strongly you felt these emotions (e.g. on a scale of 1 to 10). This will help you recognize long-term patterns.

Body scan

Close your eyes for a minute and feel into your body: Where do you feel tension? Where do you feel warmth or cold? How does your body influence your emotions? It is best to do this at a fixed time of day, for example directly after getting up or before going to bed.

Mirror technology

Observe your facial expressions and body language in different emotional states to develop a better sense of your unconscious signals. You can also record short voice memos or videos to look at yourself more objectively later.

Exercises for self-regulation

Self-regulation means controlling your own feelings and reactions in such a way that they remain in balance. This does not mean suppressing emotions but managing them constructively.

The 10-second rule

In stressful situations, consciously pause, take a deep breath and only then react. Practice this technique first in easier everyday situations (e.g. when someone is pushing in front of you in the supermarket) so that it becomes easier for you in really stressful moments.

Reframing thoughts

If you catch yourself thinking negative thoughts, consciously change your perspective: Is there a more positive or at least more neutral interpretation of the situation? Ask yourself: "How would another person I trust see this situation?"

Meditation or breathing techniques

Schedule short mindfulness exercises or breathing exercises every day to gain inner peace and more control over your emotions. Even five minutes of meditation in the morning or during your lunch break can have a positive impact on the rest of your day.

Exercises for motivation

Healthy, sustainable motivation not only helps you achieve your goals, but also gives you emotional strength in difficult times.

Create vision board

Collect pictures, quotes and symbols that represent your long-term goals and wishes. Stick them on a poster or create a digital collage. Place your vision board in a place where you can see it every day - for example at your desk or in your bedroom.

Gratitude diary

Write down three things you are grateful for every day to strengthen your positive attitude. Try to find new aspects every week and focus not only on big events, but also on small things (e.g. a smile from someone).

Self-reward system

Set yourself achievable goals and consciously reward yourself for your progress. Choose rewards that really make you happy (e.g. a good book, a relaxing bath, a trip to the movies).

Empathy exercises

Empathy means empathizing with the feelings and perspectives of others. This strengthens both private and professional relationships.

Practicing active listening

In conversations, concentrate fully on the other person, ask open questions and paraphrase what they are saying to make sure you have understood them correctly. Pay conscious attention to non-verbal signals such as tone of voice and facial expressions to gain a deeper understanding.

Change of perspective

Think about how others might feel in specific situations. Actively put yourself in their shoes and ask questions if you are unsure. In the evening, write down a situation in which you consciously tried to take the other person's perspective and what insights you gained.

Express sympathy

Write an appreciative message to a person or actively mention what you appreciate about them. In this way, you consciously perceive their feelings and respond to them. Especially in difficult phases, a small gesture of sympathy can go a long way and deepen your relationship.

Social skills exercises

Social skills include the ability to interact effectively and harmoniously with others. This includes conflict resolution, communication and an understanding of group dynamics.

Role play for difficult conversations

Practice resolving conflicts constructively with friends or colleagues by acting out certain situations. Give and receive feedback afterwards: what worked well, where could you be clearer or more empathetic?

Observe non-verbal communication

Consciously pay attention to the body language of others (posture, gestures, facial expressions) and try to interpret it. Practice this observation in everyday moments too, e.g. on the train, in a café or in meetings - but without judging, just as a silent perception.

Formulating "I" messages

Instead of reproaching ("You're always so unreliable"), express your feelings ("I feel insecure when plans are changed at short notice"). Pay particular attention to a respectful tone of voice so that the other person can remain open to your message.

Exercises for emotional intelligence in the digital world

We are also constantly interacting with others online. Emotional intelligence is therefore not only important in direct contact, but also in chats, emails and social media.

Reflect news

Read through an email or chat message again before you send it. Think about how it might come across to the recipient. Avoid ironic or sarcastic remarks in critical messages, as these can often be misunderstood in writing.

Take digital breaks

Set aside at least one day a week or several hours a day to consciously use less social media. Instead: make a phone call or meet someone in person. Turn off notifications and put your phone in another room to reduce temptations.

Consciously spreading positivity

Post a nice message, an uplifting comment or share inspiring content every day. Make sure to express genuine appreciation instead of just giving out standardized compliments - authenticity has a more lasting effect.

Reflection questions

- Which of the exercises do you find easiest? Which is the hardest?

- What changes have you already noticed by practicing regularly?

- Which exercise would you like to establish as a daily or weekly routine?

- How can you set yourself specific time slots to consistently integrate the exercises into your everyday life?

Start by choosing one or two exercises that you particularly enjoy and practice them regularly for one to two weeks. Over time, you can add more exercises. Remember that it is normal to have phases in which your motivation fluctuates. Keep at it, monitor your progress and adjust your exercise program if necessary. In this way, you will gradually lay a solid foundation for your emotional intelligence in everyday life.

To the point

- **Purpose**: EI can be trained like a muscle - by practicing regularly.
- **Exercises by competence area**:
    - Self-awareness: emotion diary, body scan
    - Self-regulation: 10-second rule, reframing
    - Motivation: vision board, gratitude diary
    - Empathy: active listening, change of perspective
    - Social skills: role-playing, ego messages
- **Integration**: Short exercises suitable for everyday use (e.g. 5 minutes of meditation).
- **Reflection questions**: Which exercise am I already doing? What would I like to try next?

Chapter 9: Your personal EI diary

Ein an EI diary helps you to become more aware of and reflect on your feelings and reactions. Regular entries will help you recognize patterns of behavior, strengths and potential for your personal development. It also helps you to reduce stress and sort out your experiences. By writing (or recording, if you prefer audio), you can name your emotions more clearly and work on your emotional intelligence in the long term.

How to keep your EI diary

Daily entries

Try to set aside a few minutes at the end of the day or several times a week to record your experiences and emotions. Continuity is the key here.

Free design

You can keep your diary handwritten in a notebook, record audio files or create a mind map. Find the style that suits you - the main thing is that you feel comfortable with it.

Honesty and openness

Allow yourself to write openly about your emotions in your diary. Don't judge yourself for certain feelings but look at them curiously and sympathetically.

Regular reflection

Look at older entries at least once a week or month. This will help you recognize progress, recurring themes and derive specific development goals.

Mia's entry in week 3

Mia started writing a few sentences in her new "EI diary" every evening three weeks ago. She felt strange at first and didn't really know what to write down. But she persevered.

In week 3, she looked back and discovered that she was particularly irritable early on some days. She wrote: "I notice that I always react irritably when I've gone to bed late and am rushed in the morning." This insight helped her to optimize her daily routine - she planned a 15-minute buffer in the morning and put her phone away earlier in the evening. "I would never have noticed without the diary," she thought. Three weeks later, she felt more relaxed overall because she recognized the warning signs in good time and took countermeasures.

Guiding questions for your EI diary

You can use these questions to help you get started:

- **What emotions did I consciously perceive today?**
  (For example, when did I feel happy, anxious, stressed or relaxed?)
- **What situations triggered these emotions?**
  (Were there specific people, places or triggers?)
- **How did I react to my emotions?**
  (And would it have been possible to react differently?)
- **Was there a moment when I was particularly empathetic?**
  (What triggered this empathy and how did it feel?)
- **What challenges have I experienced today in terms of my emotional intelligence?**
  (e.g. conflicts, difficult conversations, inner resistance).
- **What can I take away from today's experiences for the future?**
  (How do I want to react to similar situations in the future?)

If you want to examine your emotional experience more closely, it is worth observing **how your emotions manifest themselves in your body**. It is often small signals such as tension in your shoulders or neck, an accelerated heartbeat or an unusually light feeling in your head that tell you how strongly a situation is affecting you. By consciously noticing and noting these physical cues, you can sharpen your sense of your inner emotional world.

It can also be very helpful to ask yourself **what positive emotions you have consciously noticed today and what you are grateful for**. Perhaps you enjoyed the warm sun on your skin in the morning, received a little praise from a colleague or experienced an intense feeling of connection with a loved one. Gratitude directs your focus to the positive things in your everyday life and strengthens your well-being at the same time.

Finally, it is worth **reflecting** on the **thoughts** that you associate with your feelings. Are there possibly **certain beliefs** that come up again and again and influence your emotions? For example, beliefs such as "I'm not good enough" or "I always have to be perfect" could reinforce your emotional response and cause you unnecessary stress. If you become aware of such beliefs, you can question them and replace them with more beneficial beliefs if necessary. In this way, you not only learn to understand your emotions better, but also gain self-confidence and composure in dealing with them.

Advantages of an EI diary

An EI diary offers you a variety of benefits that can become noticeable after a short time. Firstly, it increases your **self-awareness** because you consciously recognize and better understand your emotions. Regularly writing them down or talking about them makes it easier to name feelings and recognize connections between triggering situations and your reaction. At the same time, this documentation specifically promotes your **EI skills**: By repeatedly recording how you acted in certain moments, you uncover potential for growth and can work more specifically on your emotional skills. Another effect is **stress reduction,** as writing down your emotions often has a liberating effect and creates clarity of thought. Finally, the EI diary contributes to your **personal development** in the long term: If you reflect regularly, you will gradually become more relaxed in dealing with stressful feelings and more empathetic towards yourself and others.

Practical implementation tips

To keep your EI diary as effectively as possible, it is helpful to designate **a fixed place and time** for your entries. Whether it's your favorite armchair or your desk - the important thing is that you feel comfortable in this place and can concentrate on your thoughts undisturbed. The time should also be well chosen, for example in the evening before you go to bed. This will quickly turn your diary into a habit that you won't want to do without.

If you want to **get creative with** your diary, feel free to try out different techniques. Perhaps you like using colors to highlight your different emotions, or you can add small drawings, symbols or collages to your entries. Such visual elements can help you express your feelings even better and recognize them later.

At the same time, **small steps are perfectly fine**. If you only have a short amount of time available, short bullet points will suffice to capture the essentials. The most important thing is regularity. Even a few brief notes can give you valuable information about how you felt in certain situations and why.

Regular review and evaluation

Regular reviews are recommended so that you can better visualize your progress. Take a look at your older entries once a month and pay particular attention to recurring patterns of behavior or emotions. Also think about what goals you would like to set yourself for the coming month: perhaps you would like to react more calmly to stressful situations or show compassion more often. And of course, it's worth keeping a written record of your progress - this positive feedback helps you to keep going and motivates you to continue working on your emotional development.

A few reflection questions can help you during this evaluation:

- What new insights have you gained from your diary?
- Have you noticed certain patterns or recurring feelings?
- Has your emotional reaction to certain situations changed over time?
- Which aspects of your emotional intelligence would you like to train more specifically?
- How do you deal with setbacks and what do you learn from them?

If you **keep** your EI diary **on an ongoing basis** and leaf through it regularly, you will notice that your awareness of your emotions and your interpersonal interactions will gradually deepen. You will recognize patterns of behavior that you may not have been aware of before and gain a clearer understanding of yourself with each entry. This is the best basis for a more mindful, satisfied and empathetic life.

To the point

- **Why**: Regular writing (or audio recordings) helps to name emotions more clearly and recognize patterns.
- **Procedure**:
    - Daily or weekly entries
    - Honest reflection on emotions, triggers, reactions
    - Answer open questions (e.g. "What made me particularly happy/stressed today?")
- **Benefits**: Increased self-awareness, stress reduction, personal growth, better overview of emotional developments.
- **Tips**:
    - Fixed place and time
    - Creative use (colors, symbols, audio notes)
    - Regular reviews (e.g. monthly)
- **Reflection questions**: Which patterns keep cropping up? What improvements do I notice?

Emotional intelligence as a lifelong journey

E Congratulations! You have gained valuable insights into the world of emotional intelligence and learned numerous practical approaches to apply it in your everyday life. You have laid the foundation for a more conscious, balanced and fulfilling life. But remember emotional intelligence is not a skill that you can acquire once and then tick off. Rather, it is an ongoing process that accompanies you throughout your life. Every day holds new challenges - and therefore new opportunities to develop your EI skills.

The most important findings from this book

Self-awareness

Helps you to consciously recognize your emotions, understand their causes and better control your reactions.

Self-regulation

Enables you to avoid impulsive behavior and direct your emotions in a targeted manner.

Motivation

Supports you in activating inner drives and pursuing long-term goals with focus.

Empathy

Is the key to deeper relationships and understanding the perspectives of others.

Social competence

Enables you to communicate clearly and appreciatively, resolve conflicts constructively and build positive relationships.

Emotional intelligence in the digital world

Encourages you to behave respectfully and empathetically online, where non-verbal signals are often lacking.

What happens next?

Maintain daily reflection

Regularly take time to question your feelings and reactions. This will help you to remain sensitive to changes and learn to take countermeasures at an early stage.

Continue the EI diary

Use your personal diary to record your progress. Write down specific situations in which you have successfully used EI strategies or experienced new challenges.

Integrate EI into new areas of life

Think about the situations in which you can use your EI skills particularly intensively - be it in your family, at work, in friendships or in voluntary activities.

Continue to learn and grow

Emotional intelligence deepens over time and with every experience. Read more books, take part in seminars or online courses and exchange ideas with like-minded people.

Using setbacks as learning opportunities

Don't be afraid to make mistakes. It is precisely from difficult situations that you will learn the most about yourself and your fellow human beings.

One last thought

Emotional intelligence is a kind of 'superpower' - it helps you to go through life more consciously, mindfully and with more compassion. It also boosts your self-awareness, makes it easier to deal with others and strengthens your mental resilience. Use the insights gained in this book as a starting point to expand your emotional competence step by step.

Thank you for embarking on this journey. May your emotional intelligence enrich you in every area of your life and help you to have authentic, fulfilling relationships - with yourself and with others.

Further reading and resources

E   Emotional intelligence is a broad field that is dealt with in various disciplines - from psychology and neuroscience to personal development. If you would like to delve deeper into certain aspects or gain new impulses, the following books and resources offer a good supplement to the contents of this book.

Classics and basics

Daniel Goleman: "Emotional intelligence: Why it matters more than IQ"

- **Why read?**
  This book is one of the cornerstones of EI. Goleman explains how emotions influence our thoughts and actions and shows why IQ alone is not enough to be successful and satisfied in life.
- **Target group**
  Readers looking for a sound introduction with a scientific background.

Daniel Goleman: "Working with Emotional Intelligence"

- **Why read?**
  Goleman's successor to the EI classic with a focus on the world of work. It clearly explains how emotional intelligence affects every day working life and what skills teams and managers need.
- **Target group**
  Especially for professionals who want to develop EI skills in a business and team context.

In-depth aspects of self-awareness and self-regulation

Tasha Eurich: "Insight: The Surprising Truth About How Others See Us, How We See Ourselves, and Why the Answers Matter More Than We Think".

- **Why read?**
  A practical book about how self-awareness develops and how we can uncover blind spots. Eurich combines research findings with easy-to-implement exercises.
- **Target group**
  Anyone who wants to deepen their self-knowledge and gain a realistic picture of themselves.

Jon Kabat-Zinn: "Healthy through meditation: The great book of self-healing"

- **Why read?**
  This classic on mindfulness and meditation provides deep insights into the conscious handling of feelings and thoughts.
  Target group
- Readers who want to explore the role of mindfulness for self-regulation and stress reduction.

Motivation and personal development

Stephen R. Covey: "The 7 Ways to Effectiveness: Principles for Personal and Professional Success"

- **Why read?**
  Although not purely a book about EI, Covey's principles (e.g. proactivity, win-win thinking) pick up on many elements of emotional intelligence. The topics of "personal responsibility" and "inner drive" in particular are vividly conveyed.
- **Target group**
  People who want to increase their personal effectiveness and self-responsibility.

Brené Brown: "Vulnerability makes you strong" (original title "Daring Greatly")

- **Why read?**
  Brown uses research and stories to show how openness and authenticity work in relationships. Vulnerability has a lot to do with self-knowledge and self-acceptance - cornerstones of EI.
- **Target group**
  Anyone who wants to free themselves from shame and perfectionism and build real self-confidence.

Empathy, social skills and relationships

Marshall B. Rosenberg: "Non-violent communication: a language of life"

- **Why read?**
  Non-violent communication" is a comprehensive concept for communicating empathetically, clearly and respectfully. The book provides concrete steps on how to recognize needs and resolve conflicts constructively.
- **Target group**
  Anyone who wants to strengthen their social skills and empathy in interpersonal relationships.

Dale Carnegie: "How to win friends"

- **Why read?**
  A classic about interpersonal relationships. Older, but still relevant when it comes to understanding others better, motivating them and winning them over.

- **Target group**
  Readers who want to approach others more consciously and are looking for timeless principles for good communication.

Digital world and modern work contexts

Travis Bradberry & Jean Greaves: "Emotional Intelligence 2.0"

- **Why read?**
  A focused look at EI training methods, especially in digital and modern work environments. Includes online tests and exercises to assess and improve your EQ.
- **Target group**
  Those who like to use practical tools and self-tests to measure their EI status.

Cal Newport: "Digital Minimalism"

- **Why read?**
  The book provides strategies on how we can use social media and digital devices more consciously. An aspect that is also important in terms of emotional intelligence in the digital space.
- Target group
  Anyone who wants to reduce digital stress and communicate more mindfully.

Further resources (online & audio)

Websites and blogs

- **Greater Good Science Center (UC Berkeley):**
  https://greatergood.berkeley.eduhttps://greatergood.berkeley.edu
  Offers articles, studies and courses on empathy, mindfulness and positive interaction.
- **Psychology Today:**
  https://www.psychologytoday.comhttps://www.psychologytoday.com
  Articles on personality, emotions and interpersonal relationships.

Podcasts

- **Brené Brown: Unlocking Us**
  Consequences around vulnerability, shame, empathy and personal growth.
- **Dan Harris: 10% Happier**
  Topics such as meditation, mindfulness and emotional well-being in everyday life.

Apps & Tools

- **Headspace or Calm (meditation apps)**
  Mindfulness and meditation exercises that help to regulate stress and strengthen self-awareness.
- **Mood tracking apps (e.g. Daylio, Moodpath)**
  Everyday companion to log emotions throughout the day and recognize patterns.

How to proceed?

Targeted selection

Think about which EI topic appeals to you the most at the moment (e.g. communication, stress management, self-awareness). Choose one or two of the books mentioned.

Deepening in small steps

Set yourself the goal of perhaps reading one chapter a week or listening to a podcast at the weekend. This will help you to continuously shape your learning process.

Putting knowledge into practice

Record important "aha" moments in your EI diary or a note app and think about how you can incorporate the new things into your everyday life.

Exchange with others

Discuss what you have read or what you have learned with friends, in a reading group or in online forums. Shared exchange deepens understanding and keeps motivation high.

These recommendations give you the opportunity to further your education depending on your focus. Whether you want to focus on empathy, strengthen your self-awareness or work on better digital communication - the literature and resources presented offer **a wide range of impulses** to deepen your knowledge and take your emotional intelligence to the next level.

Have fun discovering new ideas and approaches!

Appendix: Useful checklists for your EI trip

E Below you will find a collection of checklists to help you implement the most important EI strategies in your everyday life. Feel free to print them out or save them on your smartphone so that you don't lose track in stressful or difficult moments.

How to make the best use of these checklists

❖ Print out or save digitally.
❖ Keep them handy in a notebook, on your pinboard or in your smartphone.
  ➢ Go through regularly
  ➢ Before important conversations, during stress, when writing an e-mail or as an evening ritual (e.g. when writing a diary).
❖ Adjust points
  ➢ Adapt the checklists to your personal style. Delete points that are not relevant to you and add your own.
❖ Note progress
  ➢ Make a brief note of which points you have successfully implemented and which you found difficult. This will increase your awareness of your EI progress.

Much success using these checklists! They should help you to deal with the challenges of everyday life in a structured, mindful and more relaxed way and to deepen your emotional intelligence step by step.

Checklist for conflict discussions & role plays

Goal: To ensure that conflicts are dealt with in a fair and structured manner and to find solutions on an equal footing.

❖ **Collect facts**
  ➢ What exactly happened?
  ➢ What specific observations have I made (without interpretation or evaluation)?
❖ **Clarify your own feelings/needs**
  ➢ What do I feel in relation to the situation (e.g. anger, disappointment, insecurity)?
  ➢ What do I need or what do I hope for (e.g. clarity, respect, more trust)?
❖ **Write down the aim of the conversation and the main points**
  ➢ What do I want to achieve in the conversation (e.g. discussion, joint solution)?
  ➢ Are there any specific suggestions I would like to make?
❖ **Prepare I-messages**
  ➢ Phrases such as "I feel ... when ... because ..." instead of "You have ..."
  ➢ Be careful not to attack the other person.
❖ **Listen empathetically**
  ➢ Listen actively, ask questions, repeat: "Did I understand you correctly ...?"
  ➢ Pay attention to non-verbal signals (eye contact, nodding).
❖ **Collect solutions**
  ➢ Brainstorming with the other person: "What solutions could we try out?"
  ➢ Decide together what is realistic.
❖ **Summarize result**
  ➢ What have we agreed?
  ➢ How and when do we check whether what we have agreed works?

Checklist for reframing (self-regulation)

Goal: To consciously reinterpret negative thoughts or feelings to remain more relaxed and constructive.

- ❖ **Describe the triggering situation**
  - ➢ Short summary: "I was annoyed about ... because ..."
- ❖ **Note current thoughts/feelings**
  - ➢ Record negative things: "I think ... / I feel ..."
- ❖ **Questioning feelings**
  - ➢ Are my assumptions or assessments perhaps distorted?
  - ➢ "What proof do I actually have of ...?"
- ❖ **Looking for a new perspective**
  - ➢ "What could be positive about this situation?"
  - ➢ "What can I learn from this?"
  - ➢ "How would an outsider see it?"
- ❖ **Self-affirmation**
  - ➢ Formulate a helpful, positive statement ("I can cope", "I can do this").
- ❖ **Reflect on the result**
  - ➢ "Do I feel different now? What are my next steps?"

Checklist for digital communication (emails, chats, social media)

Goal: Communicate clearly, politely and empathetically to avoid misunderstandings.

❖ **Check subject and salutation**
  ➢ Is the subject line clear, polite and concise?
  ➢ Did I use a polite form of address ("Hello ...", "Dear ...")?
❖ **Clarity in content**
  ➢ Does my main message get straight to the point?
  ➢ Are my sentences too long or complicated?
❖ **Check tone of voice**
  ➢ Does the text appear neutral, friendly or threatening/sarcastic?
  ➢ Could something sound aggressive or reproachful?
❖ **Minimize misunderstandings**
  ➢ Use emojis or short explanations where irony/sarcasm could be misunderstood.
  ➢ Clear formulations are better than ambiguous ones.
❖ **Observe netiquette**
  ➢ Don't forget "please" and "thank you".
  ➢ Pay attention to capitalization and exclamation marks (quickly appears aggressive).
❖ **Read first, then send**
  ➢ Read texts aloud once or let them sink in briefly.
  ➢ Only then click on "Send".

Checklist for the 10-second rule & emotion control

Goal: To give yourself a moment in emotionally charged situations so that you don't act impulsively.

❖ **STOP**
  ➢ Say "stop" in your mind and take a deep breath for 10 seconds (or longer).
❖ **Body scan**
  ➢ Perceive palpitations, sweat, tension.
  ➢ Consciously relax (e.g. lower your shoulders, breathe calmly).
❖ **Naming feelings**
  ➢ "I am angry/frustrated/hurt because ..."
❖ **Reflecting on triggers**
  ➢ "What specifically triggered this? Is it something that reminds me of previous situations?"
❖ **Pause for thought**
  ➢ "What options do I have now? Do I have to answer immediately?"
❖ **Conscious reaction**
  ➢ If necessary, go out, postpone or calmly give in.
  ➢ If an answer is necessary, first-person messages or neutral statements.

Checklist for feedback meetings (professional & private)

Goal: To give or receive constructive feedback without personal attacks.

* ❖ **Define goal**
    * ➤ "Do I want to praise, constructively criticize, contribute ideas ...?"
* ❖ **Emphasize positive aspects**
    * ➤ What did the person do well? Express appreciation first.
* ❖ **Stay concrete**
    * ➤ Give concrete examples ("At the meeting I noticed that ...").
    * ➤ Avoid sweeping statements ("You are always ...").
* ❖ **Joint solution**
    * ➤ "Do you have any ideas on how we can improve this?"
    * ➤ Be open to the other person's point of view.
* ❖ **Queries**
    * ➤ Leave room for questions ("How do you see it?", "How do you feel about it?").
* ❖ **Conclusion**
    * ➤ Summarize what has been agreed ("Next time we will try out that ...").
    * ➤ Possibly make an appointment/check-in for an update.

Checklist for the EI diary (self-perception)

Goal: Regularly reflect on emotions, recognize patterns and pursue personal development.

❖ **Date and mood of the day**
  ➤ z. e.g. on a scale of 1-10.
❖ **Main events of the day**
  ➤ Key points: What was important, moving or striking?
❖ **Positive emotions & triggers**
  ➤ "What gave me pleasure? When did I feel good?"
❖ **Negative emotions & triggers**
  ➤ "What annoyed/hurt/stressed me? Why?"
❖ **Self-reflection**
  ➤ "What have I learned from this?"
  ➤ "How did I react - and how would I have wanted to react?"
❖ **Outlook**
  ➤ "What am I planning to do tomorrow/next day?"
  ➤ "Where can I specifically apply EI strategies (e.g. reframing, empathy, ...)?"

Checklist for immediate stress relief (everyday conflicts, acute stress situations)

Goal: Keep calm in acute moments of stress (whether professional or private) and remain solution oriented.

❖ **Recognize stress**
  ➢ I can tell from my body that I'm stressed (e.g. racing heart, shallow breathing)."
❖ **Short breathing space**
  ➢ Take 3-5 deep breaths or 1 minute of concentrated breathing.
❖ **Naming emotions**
  ➢ I'm angry/anxious/overwhelmed right now."
❖ **Short-term strategy**
  ➢ If possible: change room, have a drink of water, get some fresh air.
❖ **Communication**
  ➢ "Can I let others know that I need a short break right now?"
❖ **Next steps**
  ➢ "What is my next step when I am calmer?" (e.g. have a constructive conversation, create a to-do list)

Checklist for the vision board (motivation)

Goal: Create clarity about your own goals and be inspired every day.

- ❖ **Choose areas of life**
  - ➢ z. e.g. health, career, relationships, leisure, finances.
- ❖ **Targets per area**
  - ➢ 1-3 wishes or goals per topic (concrete and realistic).
- ❖ **Collect pictures and quotes**
  - ➢ Aesthetic or motivational elements that match the objectives.
- ❖ **Design planning**
  - ➢ How do I arrange pictures? Which goal is at the center?
- ❖ **Placement**
  - ➢ Hang/put in a place that you see every day (bedroom, work-place).
- ❖ **Regular updating**
  - ➢ Reflect every few months: "Are these goals still relevant? Do I need an update?"

Zeitfracht Medien GmbH
Ferdinand-Jühlke-Straße 7
99095 Erfurt, Deutschland
produktsicherheit@kolibri360.de